JUN 2 9 2019

NFL
UNDERDOG STORIES

BY JOHN TUVEY

UNDERDOG
SPORTS STORIES

SportsZone

An Imprint of Abdo Publishing | abdobooks.com

abdobooks.com

Published by Abdo Publishing, a division of ABDO, PO Box 398166, Minneapolis, Minnesota 55439. Copyright © 2019 by Abdo Consulting Group, Inc. International copyrights reserved in all countries. No part of this book may be reproduced in any form without written permission from the publisher. SportsZone™ is a trademark and logo of Abdo Publishing.

Printed in the United States of America, North Mankato, Minnesota
092018
012019

 THIS BOOK CONTAINS RECYCLED MATERIALS

Cover Photo: Tom DiPace/AP Images
Interior Photos: Nick Wass/AP Images, 5; G. Newman Lowrance/AP Images, 6; James Drake /Sports Illustrated/Getty Images, 11; Tony Tomsic/AP Images, 12; AP Images, 15; Eric Drotter/AP Images, 17; Doug Mills/AP Images, 19, 27; Ben Liebenberg/AP Images, 21; Al Messerschmidt/AP Images, 23, 41, 42; Elise Amendola/AP Images, 24; Ed Reinke/AP Images, 29; Denis Poroy/AP Images, 31, 32; Mel Evans/ AP Images, 35; David J. Phillip/AP Images, 37; Elaine Thompson/AP Images, 39; Craig Lassig/AFP/Getty Images, 45

Editor: Patrick Donnelly
Series Designer: Melissa Martin

Library of Congress Control Number: 2018949196

Publisher's Cataloging-in-Publication Data

Names: Tuvey, John, author.
Title: NFL underdog stories / by John Tuvey.
Description: Minneapolis, Minnesota : Abdo Publishing, 2019 | Series: Underdog sports stories | Includes online resources and index.
Identifiers: ISBN 9781532117633 (lib. bdg.) | ISBN 9781532170492 (ebook)
Subjects: LCSH: American football--Juvenile literature. | National Football League--Juvenile literature. | Upsets in sports--Juvenile literature. | Winning and losing--Juvenile literature.
Classification: DDC 796.33264--dc23

TABLE OF CONTENTS

CHAPTER 1

REFUSING TO QUIT

Professional football players are among the biggest people on the planet. Many were star players in college who went on to become high draft picks in the National Football League (NFL).

But the league is also filled with underdog stories. Some are smaller players who find success despite their size. Others are undrafted players who defy expectations. Some of the most famous underdogs are teams who beat the odds to win championships.

Priest Holmes played well in his few opportunities to shine with the Ravens.

Priest Holmes is one of those underdog stories. He grew up in San Antonio, Texas. In high school, despite standing just 5 feet 9 inches tall, Priest became a standout running back. He was named Offensive Player of the Year in Texas. He attended the University of Texas, but he barely played until late in his junior year. Then, in the 1994 Sun Bowl, he rushed for 161 yards. He also scored four

Holmes (31) bursts through a hole against the Chargers in 2001.

touchdowns—one more than he'd scored in his previous 24 games combined.

Holmes was set to be the Longhorns' starting running back as a senior, but he injured his knee and missed the whole season. He was granted a medical redshirt, meaning he could come back and play one more season. But when Holmes returned for his final year on campus, he had lost his starting spot to future Heisman Trophy winner Ricky Williams.

Ignored in the NFL Draft, Holmes signed as a free agent with the Baltimore Ravens. He made the team but only played on special teams as a rookie. Finally, in the fourth game of his second season, the Ravens put Holmes in the starting lineup. He rushed for 173 yards and two touchdowns. He went on to lead the team with 1,008 rushing yards on the season.

The next year, Holmes missed seven games with another injury. Also, the Ravens hired a new coach who

ROUGH STUFF

When he was growing up, Priest Holmes and his friends sometimes played football in the street. It was a rough introduction to the game. The older boys let players run along the sidewalk so they could slam them into mailboxes. Priest learned quickly how important it was to make tacklers miss!

wanted a bigger running back. So in the 2000 draft, Baltimore made bruising running back Jamal Lewis its pick in the first round. That made Holmes a backup once again, and his opportunities to play were limited.

Another player might have given up after all that adversity. But in 2001, Holmes signed as a free agent with the Kansas City Chiefs. Coach Dick Vermeil built the team's offense around him. Holmes went on to lead the NFL with 1,555 rushing yards that season.

That launched one of the most productive three-year stretches in NFL history. Holmes led the league with

21 rushing touchdowns in 2002. He boosted that total to 27 the next year, an NFL record at the time. He was named All-Pro three times and averaged 143 yards from scrimmage per game. He scored 61 touchdowns in 46 games.

Eventually injuries began to catch up to Holmes. A hard tackle led to a hip injury that ended his 2002 season two games early. A knee injury cost him half of the 2004 season. After a helmet-to-helmet hit in 2005 damaged his spinal column, Holmes played just four more games before retiring.

At every stop along the way, Holmes's team thought it could find someone to do the job better. But when he finally got a chance, he made the most of it. In the end, Priest Holmes went from undrafted free agent to the Kansas City Chiefs' Hall of Fame.

CHAPTER 2

THE GUARANTEE

The NFL and American Football League (AFL) were rival leagues that began the process of merging in 1966. For the next four years, the champions of each league met in a final game at the end of the season. That game would become known as the Super Bowl.

Because the NFL had been around much longer, most fans thought it was the better league. The NFL champion Green Bay Packers won the first two Super Bowls, easily dispatching their AFL competition. In the

Joe Namath led the New York Jets to the 1968 AFL championship.

third championship game, the NFL's Baltimore Colts were expected to do the same against the AFL champions, the New York Jets.

Leading up to the big game, all the talk was about Baltimore. After all, the Colts had just won the NFL championship with a 34–0 wipeout of the Cleveland Browns. Gamblers made Baltimore an 18-point favorite against New York. The Jets felt disrespected, and

The Jets' defense rose to the occasion, forcing five turnovers.

quarterback Joe Namath had finally had enough. At a banquet three days before the game in Miami, Namath was heckled by a Colts fan. He responded with one of the most famous lines in sports history: "We're gonna win the game. I guarantee it."

It was a bold statement from a brash young player representing an upstart league. But could he back it up?

Namath got plenty of help that Sunday. When the game began, the Colts drove the ball inside New York's 20-yard line three times in the first half. But the Jets defense held Baltimore without a point thanks to two interceptions and a missed field goal.

After the first interception, Namath drove the Jets 80 yards for a touchdown. It was the first time an AFL team held the lead in the Super Bowl.

Baltimore's problems continued in the second half. Running back Tom Matte fumbled on the first play, and New York recovered. The Jets held the ball for 12 of

COMPETITION LEADS TO COOPERATION

The NFL had been around for 40 years when the AFL started in 1960. The AFL had to pay large bonuses to lure top college players to the new league. That launched a series of bidding wars as each league tried to land the best talent. In 1966 the two leagues agreed to merge, keeping costs down and almost doubling the size of the NFL.

the 15 minutes in the third quarter, relying heavily on their own running back, Matt Snell. The Jets couldn't manage another touchdown, but they kicked two field goals to take a 13–0 lead.

Near the end of the third quarter, the Colts benched quarterback Earl Morrall, who had won the NFL's Most Valuable Player (MVP) Award. Johnny Unitas, a Hall of Fame quarterback who had been hurt most of the season, replaced Morrall.

Unitas threw a touchdown pass with three minutes left to make the score 16–7, and the Colts recovered an onside kick to get the ball back. But Unitas overthrew receiver Jimmy Orr in the end zone on fourth down, and the Jets were able to chew up enough clock to seal the massive upset.

Namath was named the game's outstanding player even though he didn't throw a touchdown pass. He had lived up to his guarantee and led the underdog Jets to a shocking Super Bowl victory.

Namath didn't have much success passing, but running back Matt Snell (41) wore down the Baltimore defense.

CHAPTER 3

BAGGING A WINNER

Kurt Warner played in three Super Bowls and was a two-time NFL MVP. But the way the quarterback's journey began, no one could have expected he would end up in the Pro Football Hall of Fame.

Big-time football schools ignored Warner's high school success, and he sat on the bench for three seasons at the University of Northern Iowa. He finally earned the starting job as a senior in 1993. Warner led UNI to the playoffs and was named the conference's Offensive Player of the Year.

Kurt Warner (13) got his first taste of professional football with the Iowa Barnstormers in the Arena Football League.

MOON MAKES HIS MARK

Warren Moon was not selected in the 1978 NFL Draft despite a standout career at the University of Washington. Moon went north, starring in the Canadian Football League. His success there led to numerous offers from NFL teams, and in 1984 he signed with the Houston Oilers. He ended up playing 17 more years with four NFL teams, throwing for 49,325 yards and 291 touchdowns. In 2006 he became the first undrafted quarterback and the first black quarterback to be inducted into the Pro Football Hall of Fame.

Yet Warner went undrafted by the NFL. The Green Bay Packers gave him a tryout, but he was cut before the season started. Warner returned to Iowa and worked nights stocking shelves in a grocery store so he could practice football during the day. He caught on with the Iowa Barnstormers of the Arena Football League and earned first-team All-Arena honors in 1996 and 1997.

Warner won the Super Bowl with the Rams in his first year as a starter.

Warner finally got his NFL shot in 1998 when the

St. Louis Rams signed him to a contract. He only threw

11 passes as a backup that year, but during the 1999

preseason, Rams starter Trent Green suffered a severe

knee injury. Warner became the Rams' starter at age 28, and the results were remarkable. He threw for 4,353 yards and 41 touchdowns and led the Rams to the Super Bowl against the Tennessee Titans. In that game, Warner threw the game-winning 73-yard touchdown pass with just over 2 minutes to go. He set a Super Bowl record with 414 passing yards and was named the game's MVP.

Two more high-flying years followed in St. Louis as Warner led the Rams back to the Super Bowl after the 2001 season. But in his first three games of 2002 he threw seven interceptions and only one touchdown pass before breaking a finger. And after he fumbled six times in the first game of 2003, he lost his starting job for good.

After one year with the New York Giants, Warner signed with the Arizona Cardinals as a short-term solution at quarterback. The Cardinals drafted former Heisman Trophy winner Matt Leinart 10th overall in 2006, and Warner and Leinart shared starting duties over the next two seasons.

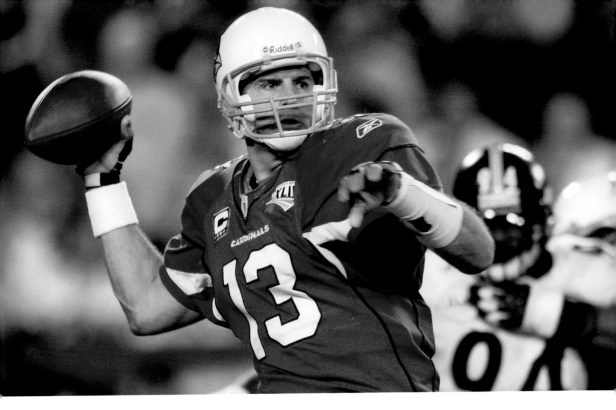

Warner led the Arizona Cardinals to the Super Bowl after the 2008 season.

In 2008 the Cardinals committed to Warner and he led them to the Super Bowl, throwing for 4,583 yards and 30 touchdowns.

When Warner retired after the 2009 season, he was one of only two quarterbacks to throw 100 or more touchdowns with two different franchises. And he's probably the only former full-time grocery clerk to be named Super Bowl MVP.

CHAPTER 4

TOM WHO?

Some dynasties have humble roots. In 2000 the New England Patriots won only five games and finished in last place in the AFC East. And the 2001 season didn't start out much better. The Patriots started 0–2. In the second game, starting quarterback Drew Bledsoe was injured by a ferocious hit. That forced New England to bring on its little-known second-year quarterback.

Fortunately for the Patriots, Tom Brady turned out to be much better than anyone expected. In Brady's first

Tom Brady was anything but a household name when he was thrust into the starting role in 2001.

NFL start, New England beat Peyton Manning and the Indianapolis Colts 44–13.

The Patriots continued to play well, improving their record to 5–4 when they met the St. Louis Rams. Head coach Bill Belichick's strategy was to focus on shutting down the Rams' MVP quarterback, Kurt Warner. His plan

Brady came up big in a blizzard to keep the Patriots' playoff push alive.

almost worked, but the Patriots couldn't quite overcome the Rams and lost by a touchdown.

New England didn't lose another game the rest of the season. The Patriots hosted the Oakland Raiders in a playoff game played in a snowstorm. Late in the fourth quarter, the Patriots tied the game on a clutch field goal by Adam Vinatieri. New England's kicker made another field goal in overtime, and the Patriots advanced to the next round.

The Patriots were 10-point underdogs to the AFC's top seed,

HUMBLE BEGINNINGS

Tom Brady started out as the seventh-string quarterback at the University of Michigan. His first college pass was intercepted and returned for a touchdown. NFL scouts thought Brady was too skinny and his arm not strong enough to be successful in the NFL. The Patriots selected him with the 199th pick of the 1999 NFL Draft, after six other quarterbacks had been selected.

the Pittsburgh Steelers. In the second quarter Brady was injured, so in a role reversal the veteran Bledsoe returned to the lineup. Then the New England special teams stepped up, returning a punt and a blocked field goal for touchdowns to help the Patriots win 24–17.

The Super Bowl brought a rematch with Warner and the Rams. St. Louis was favored by two touchdowns. But Belichick had a different defensive plan. This time his defense would focus on shutting down running back Marshall Faulk.

Belichick's plan worked. For three quarters the Patriots kept the Rams out of the end zone, and New England built a 17–3 lead. But then St. Louis scored two touchdowns in the fourth quarter to tie the game with 1:30 left.

Brady had one last chance. He led his team quickly down the field, and a 23-yard pass to Troy Brown moved the Patriots into scoring range. As time expired, Vinatieri kicked yet another clutch field goal, this time from 48 yards away, to win the game 20–17. It was the first time in history that the Super Bowl had been decided by a score on the final play of the game.

The upset win launched a New England dynasty. Over the next 16 years, the Patriots would win 14 division titles, seven AFC championships, and four more Super Bowls.

Brady's performance in the Super Bowl left no doubt who was No. 1 in the hearts of Patriots fans.

CHAPTER 5

THE GREAT GATES

The typical path to the NFL is through a big-time college football program. Some players come from smaller schools because their skills developed later. But very few players make it to the NFL without having played any college football at all.

Antonio Gates was first-team All-State in both football and basketball at Central High School in Detroit. He also helped the basketball team win a state championship

Antonio Gates played basketball at Kent State University. Football stardom came much later.

in 1998. Gates stayed close to home for college, enrolling at Michigan State University, where he hoped to play both sports. But once he arrived on campus, head football coach Nick Saban told him he had to give up basketball. Instead, Gates transferred to Eastern Michigan, but because he had fallen behind in his schoolwork, he was ineligible to play.

Gates then headed west, winding up at a community college in California where he focused on his studies and didn't play

DIAMONDS IN THE ROUGH

Where else does the NFL look for talent? Players have come from many other sports, reaching the highest level without having played college football. Renaldo Nehemiah was an Olympic hurdler who played wide receiver for the San Francisco 49ers. Stephen Neal was a college wrestler who played on the offensive line for the New England Patriots. Professional wrestler Brock Lesnar even went to training camp with the Minnesota Vikings.

either sport. Meanwhile, one of Michigan State's assistant basketball coaches took over at Kent State in Ohio. The coach contacted Gates and told him if he graduated from community college, he could come play at Kent State.

Gates accepted the offer and joined the Kent State basketball team. The 6-foot-4 power forward helped Kent State reach the Elite Eight of the National Collegiate Athletic Association (NCAA) tournament his junior year, and as a senior he was an honorable mention All-American.

Most pro basketball scouts thought Gates was too short to play

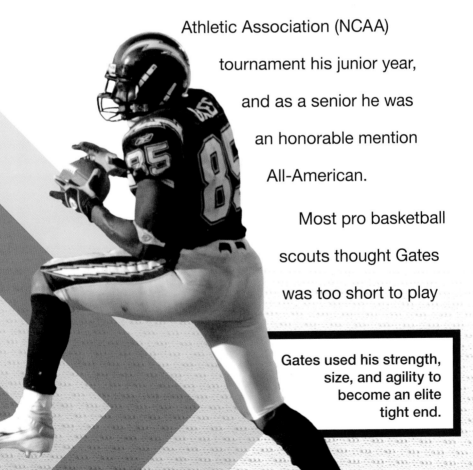

Gates used his strength, size, and agility to become an elite tight end.

his position in their league. But the NFL's San Diego Chargers thought his height and quickness would make him an ideal tight end, so in 2003 they signed him as a free agent.

Though he hadn't played football in five years, Gates cracked the Chargers' starting lineup as a rookie. His success was almost immediate. He made the Pro Bowl the

Gates liked to pay tribute to his basketball roots when he celebrated a touchdown catch.

next year, the first of eight straight trips to the NFL's annual all-star game.

Gates quickly became quarterback Philip Rivers's favorite target. The two teamed up for 87 touchdowns, more than any other quarterback-tight end combination in NFL history.

Over his first 15 years with the Chargers, Gates caught 927 passes for 11,508 yards. Those are team records, as well as the third-highest totals for a tight end in NFL history. In 2017 Gates passed Hall of Famer Tony Gonzalez to set an NFL record for most touchdown catches by a tight end with 114.

Gates put up his impressive numbers at the highest level of his sport despite having played zero games of football in college. He is an example of how NFL teams often find talented players beyond the usual places.

CHAPTER 6

KILLER GIANTS

The 2007 New York Giants didn't exactly get off to a great start. They lost their first two games, giving up 45 points to the Dallas Cowboys and 35 points to the Green Bay Packers.

But a goal-line stand in a win against Washington the following week helped the Giants turn their season around. New York went 10–6 and clinched a spot in the playoffs heading into the final regular season game. In Week 17 the Giants faced the New England Patriots, who were 15–0

The Giants were searching for answers after starting the 2007 season with two disappointing losses.

and hoping to complete a perfect regular season. The Giants battled but ended up losing 38–35.

Because they were a wild card team, the Giants had to play on the road in the playoffs. In the first round they went to Tampa Bay and beat the Buccaneers 24–14 behind two touchdown passes from quarterback Eli Manning. The next week they faced the top-seeded Dallas Cowboys, who had beaten the Giants twice already that season. New York's defense stood strong and led the Giants to a 21–17 upset.

In the conference championship game, the Giants had to battle two opponents—the Green Bay Packers and the sub-zero temperatures in Wisconsin. Again, it was the defense leading the way, as cornerback Corey Webster intercepted a Brett Favre pass early in overtime. Four plays later, Lawrence Tynes redeemed himself after missing two field goals in the fourth quarter. Tynes booted a 47-yard field goal through the uprights, and the Giants were headed to the Super Bowl with a 23–20 victory.

Lawrence Tynes (9) and holder Jeff Feagles celebrate the Giants' frigid victory over the Packers.

Their final opponent would be the mighty Patriots. New England was trying to become the first NFL team to go 19–0 in a season. The Patriots were favored to win by as much as two touchdowns.

The New York defense kept the pressure on Patriots quarterback Tom Brady all game, sacking him five times. New England's top-ranked offense had just one touchdown to its credit until late in the game. Then Brady threw a 6-yard touchdown pass to Randy Moss to give the Patriots a 14–10 lead with less than three minutes to play.

The Giants responded with two first downs, moving the ball out to their 44-yard line with 1:15 to play. Facing third down and 5 yards to go, Manning dropped back to pass.

The Patriots almost sacked him—one linebacker even had Manning's jersey in his hand—but Manning ducked away and spun to his right.

Free from the pass rush, Manning heaved the ball downfield, where wide receiver David Tyree and safety Rodney Harrison of

OH BROTHER

Eli Manning was named the MVP of the Super Bowl victory over the Patriots. He earned the same honor four years later when the Giants once again defeated Brady and the Patriots in the Super Bowl. That moved him one trophy ahead of his older brother, Peyton, who was named the MVP when the Indianapolis Colts beat the Chicago Bears in the Super Bowl after the 2006 season.

the Patriots leaped for the ball. Tyree pinned the ball to his helmet to hold on as the two players fell to the ground at the New England 24.

Four plays later, Manning threw a 13-yard touchdown to Plaxico Burress to give the Giants a 17–14 lead with 39 seconds to go. New York's defense stood up to the Patriots one last time, and the upset was complete. The Giants had ended the Patriots' hopes for a perfect season.

New York's defense kept the Patriots in check long enough for the Giants' offense to mount a game-winning drive.

CHAPTER 7

BIG HEART, BIG TALENT

John Randle was raised in Mumford, Texas, in a two-room shack with no running water. As a kid, John liked football, but he almost quit his high school team because after practice he had to hitchhike back home. Some days he didn't get home until after midnight. John's mother encouraged him to stick with football, so he could earn a college scholarship like his older brother, Ervin.

Ervin played football at Baylor University. But John didn't have the grades to qualify at a Division I college.

John Randle was known as much for his boisterous personality as for his ability to sack the quarterback.

He started out at a two-year school where he was a junior college All-American as a defensive lineman. He moved on to tiny Texas A&I, where he earned Little All-America honors.

However, he was ignored in the 1990 NFL Draft. The 6-foot-1 Randle was short for his position, and he had a hard time keeping weight on. Ervin Randle, who was playing for the Tampa Bay Buccaneers, got him a tryout with the team. But the Buccaneers wanted to move him to linebacker, so

Randle's quickness allowed him to leave would-be blockers in the dust on his path to the quarterback.

he left. After another unsuccessful tryout with the Atlanta Falcons, Randle ended up in Minnesota.

A Vikings assistant coach told Randle if he weighed 250 pounds the team would give him a chance. At the time, Randle only weighed 244 pounds, so he bought a thick chain at a hardware store and tied it around his waist under his jersey. When he got on the scale, he weighed just enough to get that chance.

STICKING WITH IT

Linebacker James Harrison went undrafted out of Kent State in 2002. He was cut by the Steelers and Ravens during his first two years out of college. He considered retiring to become a bus driver. But he finally stuck with the Steelers in 2004 and became a starter. In 2008 Harrison set a team record with 16 sacks and became the only undrafted player ever to win the Defensive Player of the Year Award.

As a rookie, Randle played on special teams and worked on techniques to help him defeat bigger opponents. He learned how to use his hands to fight off blockers and how to use his speed to spin around them. He also benefitted from working against future Hall of Fame offensive guard Randall McDaniel every day in practice.

Randle cracked the starting lineup in his second season with the Vikings. In 1992 he began a streak of eight straight seasons with double-digit sacks. The six-time All-Pro led the NFL with 15.5 sacks in 1997.

Many offensive linemen were intimidated by Randle, and not just because he was so good. He often painted his face with eye black. A notorious trash talker, he also liked to learn personal information about his opponents that he could use to distract them during the game.

The durable Randle didn't miss a game in his first 11 NFL seasons. By the time his 14-year career was

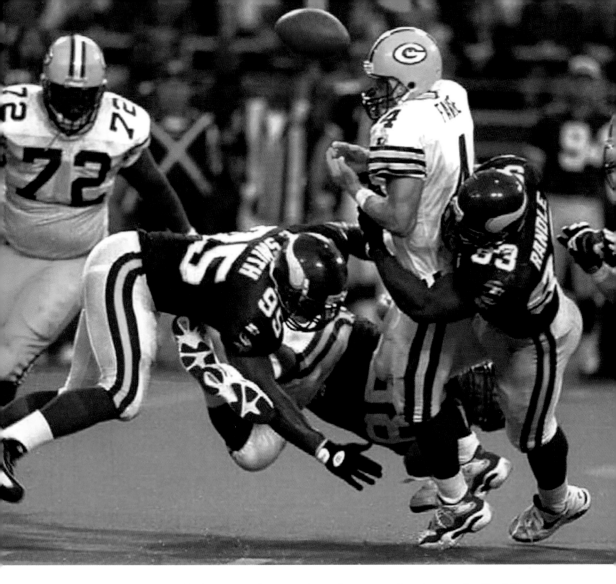

Randle (93) particularly enjoyed tormenting future Hall of Fame quarterback Brett Favre (4) when the Vikings played the Packers.

finished, he had amassed 137.5 quarterback sacks. That was tied for fifth all-time when he retired in 2003. He was named to the NFL's All-Decade team of the 1990s, and in 2010 he was elected to the Pro Football Hall of Fame.

GLOSSARY

draft

A system that allows teams to acquire new players coming into a league.

dynasty

A team that has an extended period of success, usually winning multiple championships.

free agent

A player whose rights are not owned by any team.

goal-line stand

A defensive stop on a play or multiple plays that begin just outside the end zone.

onside kick

A kickoff that is purposely short with the hope that the kicking team can recover the ball.

overtime

An extra period of play when the score is tied after regulation.

sack

A tackle of the quarterback behind the line of scrimmage before he can pass the ball.

special teams

The players on the field for kicking and punting plays.

wild card

A team that makes the playoffs even though it did not win its division.

MORE INFORMATION

BOOKS

Graves, Will. *The Best NFL Offenses of All Time.* Minneapolis, MN: Abdo Publishing, 2014.

Myers, Dan. *NFL's Top 10 Plays.* Minneapolis, MN: Abdo Publishing, 2018.

Wilner, Barry. *Tom Brady vs. Joe Montana.* Minneapolis, MN: Abdo Publishing, 2018.

ONLINE RESOURCES

Booklinks
NONFICTION NETWORK
FREE! ONLINE NONFICTION RESOURCES

To learn more about NFL underdog stories, visit **abdobooklinks.com**. These links are routinely monitored and updated to provide the most current information available.

INDEX

ABOUT THE AUTHOR

John Tuvey has written about sports for publications and websites as small as his hometown newspaper and as big as *USA Today*. He graduated from St. John's University in Collegeville, Minnesota, where he also played football for legendary coach John Gagliardi. Tuvey grew up in Janesville, a small town in southern Minnesota, where his dad coached him in football, basketball, and track and field. He now lives in St. Paul, Minnesota, and stays involved in sports by cheering on his four children.